THE
NEEDS
OF THE
HEART

THE SECOND ROOT *of*
THE SPIRITUAL ROOT SYSTEM™

CHIP DODD

SAGE HILL RESOURCES

624 Grassmere Park Drive, Suite 11
Nashville, TN 37211

www.sagehillresources.com

CONTENTS

⚭

THE
NEEDS
of the
HEART

INTRODUCTION

CR

The Spiritual Root System™ is comprised of five sections: feelings, needs, desire, longings, and hope. *The Voice of the Heart* is an in depth presentation of our feelings: what they are, where they come from, how to live with them, and how they are integral to living a full life. As the five areas of our lives that comprise the Spiritual Root System™ lead into each other, acknowledging and expressing our feelings awaken us to our needs in a significant way. The following material presents the primary needs of a human being. It elucidates them, shows how to go about living these needs, and describes the process by which living in need leads us into relationship with ourselves, others, and God.

The most difficult part about needs is that we can do rational gymnastics over the top of them; we can anesthetize, repress, suppress, deny, and depress our needs. The way we go about avoiding our needs often leads to negative survival outcomes: we practice impaired forms of attempting to live fully without having to feel fully. Addictive processes, reactive self-sufficiency, and forms of obsessive and compulsive self-cures begin as forms of self-protection when we deny that we have needs. These self-protective survival skills do, indeed, defend us from "getting hurt" at first, but eventually become self-destructive to relationship with our selves, others, and God because we become defended against all pain that is inevitable to truly being alive and loving. Simply put, we are capable of ignoring our needs, but we are unable to escape them.

The scariest and most vulnerable part about admitting our neediness is that we or someone else can always tell us that we are "making it up" or that we "should not" have that particular need. The difficult truth is that no matter how strongly we align with the world's demands that we not be needy, we are structured emotionally and spiritually to have needs; again, they can always be suppressed, but never evaded completely. Although we can rationalize our way away from our needs, I have taught for many years that, "Wherever I go, there I am." There is no such place as "away," i.e., a place where we do not have feelings, needs, desire, longings, and hope. There really is no place I can go to escape my self. Therefore, to live well, I must face my self.

Facing, or even accepting, that there is no such place as away from our feelings and needs provides a spring board for taking the risk of turning around and facing how we are made. When we risk acknowledging our needs, we discover that we have been running from who we are created to be for quite some time.

Of course, this idea begs the question: Who are we created to be? I believe that we really are born to become certain kinds of people. The core from which we are created to express ourselves is emotional and spiritual, which renders us capable of living fully in relationship; we are made to simultaneously be integrated and yet unique, to be connected and yet separate. Human beings have three primary relationships that are integral to living fully. The first relationship is with our selves. When lived in a healthy way, this relationship can be as simple as recognizing, accepting, and responding out of how we are created. Secondly, we are created to participate in relationships with others. Relationships with our neighbors are built on the acknowledgment that we are needy emotional and spiritual creatures who are unable to find fulfillment without receiving from and giving to each other.

Finally, we are created for a relationship with God. A relationship with God begins by engaging with the reality that we are not in control of our lives, and believing in a God who is faithful to our hearts. We have a God who we can cry out to who meets us in our needs. When we are able to experience these three relationships through our feelings and needs, we find ourselves in the midst of a full life. When we live in full relationship, we do not protect ourselves from needing, which isolates us. Instead, we participate fully in living, which creates an outcome of having a security that offers others the safety of being in need, too.

If we are created as emotional and spiritual creatures, how do we so often manage to stray from our createdness? Why do we run from our emotional and spiritual cores? More often than not, we run away from who we are, because we get told that something is wrong with how we are made—we *should* be something and someone else. Our parents, peers, coaches, directors, and other teachers tell us that we need to *do* something rather than *be* someone, which sets up the difficult position of having to perform rather than be fully present. We often remain obedient to who people told us we *should* be—even to the point of our own self-destruction—in the hope that we can earn the right to have our needs met some day.

When we live our lives running from who we are, when we remain obedient to those people who teach and demand that we abandon the core of who we are, we spend our lives in a make believe place called "some day." I'll say it again, when we run from who we were created to be, we spend our lives trying to do something we were not created to do—earn the right to have needs. If you tell a fish to climb a tree, it will spend its whole life despising itself for not being able to do what it was not created to do. We are taught to despise our selves for being, at core, emotional and spiritual creatures who must have certain needs met in order to live fully. We can survive our whole lives with these unfortunate, mistaken beliefs. And miss the living.

Thirty years ago I did not believe that needs mattered. I did not even know what they were. In fact, beyond biological needs, I denied my richer needs absolutely, and walked away from being told about healthy needs. I was trapped in the addictive process of doing whatever was necessary, through self-sufficiency, to avoid the vulnerability of needing. Thirty years ago a person asked, "What are your needs?" I remember that I looked back in my mind, and recalled a psychology class from high school or college. I remembered some of Maslow's theories about what people must have in order to survive: food, shelter, clothing, and water. I remember thinking, "Got it," and I told this person about my needs based on my memory of Maslow. She replied, "Well, okay, what else do you need?" I had no further answers to give her. At this point in my life, I considered anything beyond food, water, clothing, and shelter a luxury. Does this sound familiar to you?

Thirty years ago I began to awaken. I had been rendered foolish by denial about and contempt towards how I was created. I believed every word of what I told this person. I believed that my greatest strength was not needing help; how ironic that my greatest "need" was not to need at all. I thought that strength was willpower—my power to will my core self away. I didn't know that what I thought of as my greatest strength functioned to help me run away from the vulnerability of feeling and needing. I just thought that if I had a problem, I'd figure it out; I believed that if I figured hard enough and long enough, I'd get it done. I believed that if I couldn't find the solution, then I had failed personally. I did not know that I was sick. I did not know that what I thought of as strength was deadly.

If we run from our needs, from the people we are created to be, we have to find ways to ignore our emotional and spiritual cores. Our emotional and spiritual cores can only be ignored over time by becoming addicted to self-sufficiency and/ or self-cures. Addictions operate in the parts of our lives we have to suppress (feelings, needs, desire, longings, and hope) in order to maintain the belief that we can overcome our struggles through willpower, thinking, and performance (a distorted form of morality). Essentially, addiction is an attempt to have a full life without having to feel fully. Our self-cures, our drugs of choice, range from conquering someone, to drugs and alcohol, having command over people, to sex, accomplishment, performance, approval and the list goes on. An addiction is an obsessive and/or compulsive "anything" that keeps us away from the core of who we are created to be and, by doing so, slowly kills us. Our addictions cover up our feelings and needs, which are the areas of our lives that if left unattended, we wither and die. The effects of our addictions also have consequences that reach far beyond the effect upon one's own life. Because we are relational, others are also profoundly affected.

Our needs are so powerful that they are somehow—even in the most stringent, strangulated way—going to be met. For example, imagine some geraniums are placed in an attic or a cellar in an attempt for them to survive the winter. By the time you get them out in the spring, the little tendrils that survive through sheer "desire" are almost translucent from lack of proper nourishment; they have reached towards whatever light they can find in order to survive. Your needs are similar. Needs are going to be met somehow, even if the form is an impaired, strangulated way. If you can't face them, counterfeit solutions take the place of legitimate needs. The impaired forms of getting needs met become the addictive processes.

CHAPTER 1

WHAT IS A NEED?

☙

Being alive is hard and it hurts. The less we run from our lives (our selves) and begin to face how we are made, the more we will begin to feel the aches and pains, the devastation and despair, of living on the Earth. If we become committed to living from our emotional and spiritual cores, then we have to know how to stop and heal from the wounds that life inflicts and/or the "emptying" that daily life demands. To put it as starkly as possible, a need is a deficit that requires biological, emotional, and spiritual gratification for fulfillment. Needs are the tools we have been given to receive healing, replenishment, and recovery, so that we can press onward toward being and expressing who we were created to become.

In order to find the strength to live a full life, we are made to have a replenishing resource of people in our lives and a God that meet us in the midst of life's turmoils. The most important step in living a full life is to become good at being needy. Neediness is something that we have to practice; we become good at being needy over time—even though we were experts at needing at birth. In order to be met in our places of need, we have to confess our needs to our selves, others, and God. When we face our selves, we discover that we are unable to fulfill our needs on our own. Our sources of strength fall outside of our selves; we are relational creatures. Neediness is the paradoxical doorway to the strength we were created to have.

We use our needs to respond to the courses our lives take, so that we have strength to face our desire, longings, and hope. Our needs are present to enhance the relational ability of the human being, which is the source of our greatest strength. We gain strength to face and feel our lives from relationships that are lived connected to our emotional and spiritual centers. The true needs of the human being are relational, not primarily biological. Furthermore, our truest relational needs are so important that they must be fulfilled, or we will die an emotional and spiritual death. For a simple illustration, imagine that someone plants me in the ground up to my waist. If they give me food, water, comfortable temperatures, and sun, I will plop over in a few hours (though the super-tough may last a couple of days). Water, sun, and dirt are not the sustenance needs that have to be met in order for you to grow into who you are made to be. Our emotional and spiritual needs involve needing someone to be with us, to help us out, to rescue us, to touch us, to find us, and to seek us out. We are created to be planted in relationships and grow into life.

HOW DO WE BEGIN LIVING IN NEED?

Living our needs starts with confession. Confession means to agree that I am human, that I am full of feelings and needs. Our needs will never be met unless we become human in order to have them met. Simply, living in need starts out with us admitting we have them. If we don't admit our needs—what I call living in refusal—we spend our lives using others as a drug that allows us to hide from how we are made. When we live in refusal, we spend our lives trying to figure others out, so we can use them as counterfeit fulfillments. Many couples spend a lot of time trying to demand the other figure out and anticipate their needs, so neither has to face and confess them. Beginning to live out of our emotional and spiritual cores involves living in confession of our feelings and needs with those we love, rather than spending our lives trying to figure each other out and survive. No one can "fix" us, but others and God can meet us in our needs.

☙

To this point, we have discussed how our needs can be ignored and how living a full life requires that we face them. We can run from our emotional and spiritual cores through the use of self-sufficiency and self-cure actions that become addictive processes. These processes allow us to escape the feelings, needs, desire, longings, and hope that we are born with. Facing our feelings and needs leads us into a level of relationship that becomes our greatest source of strength to live lives of passion and thanksgiving. Remember, our needs are more relational than strictly biological, so things like food and water do not make my list. Living fully requires that we become confessors of our needs to our selves, others, and

God. Now, we move to defining and discussing some of our specific needs and how to move along the path of living them in daily life.

CHAPTER 2

BELONGING

CR

The need to belong is one of the two of our most powerful needs; the other is the need to matter, which is discussed next. Belonging is the need to be accepted for who we are as emotional and spiritual beings. In order to find belonging, we have to know how to both confess our needs and how to be met in the confession of our needs by trusted others, to be accepted for being human. The need to belong matters more than food, water, shelter, and clothing. A child will walk away from a table of food, so to speak, to find the parent. This is a literal metaphor, illustrating that the child will leave food to find a more important sustenance. What happens to the child's need to belong when the child's powerless humanity is consistently rejected by the parent? Simply, the child will begin to be ashamed of their need of others, and their desire to find "someplace" to belong.

As I said earlier, many of us are taught to despise our neediness, because our needs often go unmet. What's the first thing we often do when we start to despise our humanity? We run from being known in our vulnerability, because we carry a message inside us that tells us that there is something wrong with having feelings and needs. We learn to think that if others know us, they will: reject us, run away, not like us, find something wrong with us, start a fight with us, judge us, own us, enslave us, indebt us, and so on. We also hide ourselves because our need to belong has been exploited and tyrannized by unhealthy others, leading to the aforementioned legitimate list of reasons why we try to escape our need to be known. However, once we begin to face the reality that there is no such place as away from our feelings and needs, we can start engaging with our need to belong, because we cannot stop believing that there is a place on the earth where we can be accepted for being human.

Again, the need to belong is the need to be accepted for being you; belonging is being accepted for being human. If this need is not met, we will search externally through performance throughout our lives for an internal security we will not find. Being you begins with the ability to live in the confession of your feelings and needs. The beginning of living fully is bringing the desperation of hope that we belong somewhere and the courage to express it through confession. Living in confession means bringing the feelings, needs, desire, longings and hope we have within us to the possibility of trusting another person. Living in the world of belonging means: to be delighted in, trusting someone to be curious about us, allowing someone to stand in our way, and permitting someone to be in pain with us. Life in a place where we belong is where a life of love is experienced and lived out.

CHAPTER 3

MATTERING

⟨⟩

I find it beneficial to begin describing the need to matter with a simple example from modern science that my patients have taught me. Based upon the DNA of human beings, we're approximately 99.9% the same. We are .01% unique. Take a moment to ponder the power of that .01%. Not a single one of us looks the same, acts the same, thinks the same, and yet we are remarkably similar in what we need in order to thrive. Just as cellular life functions similarly in us, so does our emotional and spiritual makeup. What a great stew we can have if we combine everything together, if we commit to continually expressing our .01%. To put it as plainly as possible, mattering is being appreciated for the .01% that's unique to us and is an expression of our uniqueness. Joined with others, we have the musical giftedness to create a very complex and astounding symphony.

While the need to belong is finding a place where we can be human together, the need to matter is met through being appreciated for our individual gifted-ness—what is born into us that comes out of us, and is developed. Any place we belong would be different without our particular expression of uniqueness. The need to matter is the need to be appreciated, cared about, and related to in the singularity that we are. Mattering is being cherished for what we bring through confession, not a product we can make and give to other people.

I will say it again, mattering is not a performance-based product. The need to matter is not met through being acknowledged based on test scores, financial portfolios, surgical cases, high school soccer goals, or great dancing. Mattering is being valued by trusted others for the continual expression of our core selves—our feelings, needs, desire, longings, and hope and what is created out of them. We know we are being met in our need to matter when we become confident that what we bring through our personal expression of our particular passions adds to our community of belonging.

So, we have the need to belong and the need to matter. These are the needs that take primacy over all the other needs. Without these two being met, the other ones cannot be met, because there is no opening for us to trust others to the extent that we can become vulnerable enough to have our other needs engaged with. This is why the capacity to be needy, to admit that we are human, can only be engaged in what I call a Circle of Security. Circles of Security are communities of people that gather together to live in confession based on the shared need of others and God. Finding a place to belong and matter allows us to begin engaging our other needs that can safely be confessed because we have others with us who we can trust with our lives.

CHAPTER 4

SECURITY

CR

The next need—and the following are not in descending order of importance—is the need for security. The need for security is met by having a "place" where we can struggle and be supported in that struggle. I use "place" because security can involve others, God, and/or even a literal space. Concerning struggle in this "place," we are free to wrestle with our selves without having to watch out for "the critic"— the inner/outer critic; we truly do not have to arrive at answers while we wrestle with our questions; we know that we will not be shamed, rejected, judged, or controlled for the vulnerability we display.

At the same time, we can be met with feedback that can be painful. This feedback can be received, because the others in the group are trusted to want what is best for us. Security offers safety while we express the "dangerous" substance of not being focused on others' needs at the moment. Security is a relational "place" where we are able to struggle with just simply being where we are at the given moment. Is it not amazing that security is actually a place to struggle through expressing vulnerability? A secure "place" is one to go to and be insecure, genuinely insecure, which is the admission of our needs. Security needs are met in the "place" where we find other people who will be with us as we struggle to confess and live our humanity.

Along with being able to struggle, security is also a "place" where we will be upheld, supported. The people/space/God in true Circles of Security are strong enough to deal with us. In other words, they know what it's like to struggle with being human, so they are able to tolerate our humanity. They have security, so they can offer security. So, in a simple metaphor, security is a place we run to when we become lacking in our sense of "place," where we can find the freedom to be in a struggle, and the faith that in this "place" we will be upheld in our neediness. In this experience, we find strength to re-enter a world that will empty us.

Now, and this is an important point, security does not provide a "place" for us to make demands on others that we be fixed from having to need. Demanding that we be fixed involves pseudo-struggling out loud with the goal of others making us "bullet-proof." Anyone who would offer such a guarantee seeks power over us in a trade-off for the mistaken belief that one will never have to feel or need again.

Therefore, the need for security is twofold. We have the need to be able to be with a group of people who can bear our struggle for life, which means we have a "place" to go be insecure. Along with having a place to be insecure, we are secure when we have faith that we will be upheld by trusted others. When secure, we believe that we can come apart without falling to pieces, as we have faith that others will be with us in our struggle for life.

CHAPTER 5

TOUCH

℞

The need for touch is one of the deepest forms of fulfillment that we have, and it can be one of the most abused needs that we possess. The touch of nurturing is such an integral, inborn emotional and spiritual need that a child can fail to thrive without it; that is, the child will literally not develop physically according to developmental norms without being touched well. We need more than custodial care to thrive and to become empathic human beings. Food, water, shelter, and clothing are not the true prerequisites to develop into a fruitful human being. Biological provision produces survival and can enhance production—the same way trees, slugs, and cattle develop. Meeting the needs of the emotional and spiritual person, however, can create thriving and growing courageous, empathic, and decisive human beings who can experience others as more than a provisional food source! They see others as carrying the same needs as themselves and, therefore, will have a tendency to have personal kinship identification—care.

Emotional growth and trust are connected to touch if we're touched well. We are created to receive (and, of course, offer) touch in certain ways based upon the relational intimacy and age appropriateness that we have with people in our lives. For example, if a loved one comes over to you and places his or her hands on your shoulders briefly, and then moves on with a soft pat, you may experience an inner-warmth that feeds the connection you have with that person or even grows the connection with that person. In addition, your need for belonging and mattering was fed through the brief moment of appropriate, caring touch. You have absorbed into your heart the food that grows many results: trust, the ability to ask questions, to access more needs, awakening of care, a sense of well-being, the courage to carry on, the awareness of how much you need assurance and have missed it; allows the voice of deeper needs, the courage to speak; opens the heart to favorable memories or the deficit of favorable memories. I give all these examples as a shorthand statement to illuminate the power and potential of touch to expand our worlds. I also give the bundle of examples to allow the reader to infer how the abuse of touch can create its converse—the distrust of connection that is trustworthy, empathic, and giving.

Touch is a non-lingual communication that connects with the heart's hunger for security, mattering, belonging, and the desire to be cared about and to express care. The need for genuine, appropriate touch bears meaning and expresses craving for life beyond words; its abuse is, likewise, monumental. For example, the world of pornography reveals and parodies the power and need for touch and its abuse, as it is a world of touch that does not grow the heart. It may momentarily satiate the body, yet it leaves the heart untouched and ignored. I believe that we carry much shame about our need to be touched, and, therefore, much denial related to the deeper, richer sustenance of touch.

Attempting to get our need for touch met in a fashion that will hide shame, reinforce denial, and protect the heart from risk leads to a multitude of non-relational ways that we receive "touch" that aim to dodge the vulnerability that our need exposes. Whatever blocks us from the awareness of our neediness and of another knowing my neediness leads to an existence centered around survival; the attempt to get my needs met without vulnerability becomes that which can block touch from reaching the place where it can deliver its healing balm and encourage strength.

CHAPTER 6

GRIEF

CR

Human beings actually have a need to grieve. We carry within us the capacity to process loss and, by doing so, experience subsequent perseverance. The process of grief honors loss by facing and going through the process of feeling a broken attachment. Change has occurred. When a connection is broken, our hearts are pulled sharply, and we have pain— leaving us with the need to grieve.

Life is more full of loss than anything else. Even if you came from a perfect childhood, you do not live there anymore. That is a loss. And by the time we are a certain age, we begin to face things we will never be able to do in our futures. Growing up we dreamed about "the someday" when we were going to do a certain thing, or go to a certain place, or that life would turn out a certain way. Even if we achieved many of the fulfillments we strove towards, we must leave them eventually—everything ends. Time itself passes and takes us with it. If we attempt to live a "smaller" life in an effort to reduce our losses and griefs, we will miss everything we are made to reach for. We need to grieve.

And yet, if we acknowledge our need to grieve, if we surrender to the process of loss, we find that we are, at the great risk of sounding trite, okay. We are okay not because we ran from our grief, but because we let ourselves grieve the truth of our hope and cares, loves and memories. We let our lives matter to our hearts and we let our selves belong to life. We attached. Every attachment (1) increases the evidence and experience of caring, (2) expands the experience of living fully, (3) increases the risk of loss and pain, (4) and guarantees the result of pain. (5) If we can permit ourselves the gift of sadness, we release that sadness by honoring the attachment that is "gone." (6) When we grieve, we release our losses with care and speak to that care; in so doing, we honor them by living and loving again. Any loving parent, as they age and move towards death wishes to be missed, because the attachment in the relational living is broken. Moreover, this parent would wish that the loved one continue onward into life with memory and vibrancy for living still. Our ability to grieve allows us to face the passing of time, in all of its effects, and re-enter life to persevere in the present with hope for the future.

Being able to grieve frees us to take the risk of celebrating.

As stated above, an integral part of the need to grieve is its connection to our capacity to care. It is also closely connected to our ability to celebrate—the opposite of grief on the continuum of living. Being able to grieve frees us to take the risk of celebrating, to be present in all of life. Willingness to grieve allows us to live fully between the polarities of celebration and grief, where we were created to live with courage. We are often told to calm down and quit celebrating, or to quit crying and get over our grieving. If we stop celebrating our love of life, we will also have to reject the need to grieve, and in so doing, reduce our ability to live life fully. Reduce grief, reduce attachment; reduce care, reduce celebration; reduce living, and, thus, reject creation.

A full life is lived in between grief and celebration. People who cannot grieve fully will never celebrate completely. If we are not willing to grieve, not willing to feel the pain of loss, we will have to protect ourselves from having the full joy of the moment and the gratitude of gain. How ironic that one of the most personally threatening things we can do is express the courage to care about something/somewhere/someone and celebrate it. What happens when we celebrate? We temporarily forget that life is full of loss. We forget for a while that loss can happen. And then, if we cannot tolerate grief, we say when loss comes our way, "What a fool I was for celebrating, for believing there was goodness in life!" We have contempt for allowing ourselves to live.

Grief opens the door to being loved.

In contrast, if we can grieve well, we will live euphorically. Euphoria means to bear life well. If we can love in the midst of knowing that we can lose this person or this passion, what a treasured experience the daily life with the beloved is. Every day we choose them, knowing that our time on the earth is limited, no matter what. Every day we can find gratitude to be with them. And then when they are gone, we know that we were fully present while life was happening. The only way to be present with the beloved is to be able to live in the midst of grief and celebration.

Not only do we need to grieve, we also need the opportunity to grieve. This notion brings us back to the Circle of Security. How many of us feel the need to apologize the moment we begin to cry in the company of other people? When we cry, in our fear of rejection, we often say things like, "Hey, I'm sorry. I'm sorry to bother you. I didn't mean to burden you. I'm sorry." Somewhere and somehow the opportunity to do what is normal in life—allow ourselves to be cared about or care about someone else—became wrong. This shame robs us of the capacity to live fully. When we find groups who are able to bear life well together, over time we lose the need to apologize for struggling out loud with our lives. The struggle becomes what brings us closer together as we continually face our selves and share our feelings and needs with trusted others. Grief opens the door to being loved; celebration opens the door to offer love.

CHAPTER 7

ATTENTION

CR

The need for attention is something that we are often told we need to get over somewhere between the ages of 10-14 years of age. If you haven't gotten over your need for attention by 18 or 19, then you are a baby, i.e., you have a great deal of growing up to do, and cannot be trusted until you don't need attention. On the contrary, attention is actually something we need throughout our lives. Attention is for grown-ups. In fact, the more we offer to life as we age, the more attention we need. Those who give more of themselves actually need more attention. And they must be responsible for knowing their needs, the denial of which can cause significant, unnecessary harm to one's self and others.

Attention means to be recognized, tended to, cared for, and even nurtured, so that we can re-experience the encouragement that comes from knowing we belong and matter. Most literally, attention means that the person in need is heeded, a word rarely used, yet it fits so well. Heeding someone's needs means close, concentrated, considerate focus upon that person. One who is in need of tending truly needs to be heeded. Heeding someone is like a doctor bringing care and competence to the patient in order to bring the person to full health. Except in the need for attention, the one in need is not sick; the person in need is fully human. Remember, emotional and spiritual needs do not expose sickness; they acknowledge shared humanity. Our sickness often originates in the denial of our needs.

In order to be tended to, we have to know (experience with our senses) our human limits and recognize our needs. If we live in refusal of our needs, they will become demands on others to fix us for being tired and weary. Because the need for attention is both often deeply denied by adults, and specifically caregivers; and because we are taught to see the need for attention as shameful, I remind the reader of its importance and its "inner-insistence" to be addressed. If we do not confess our need for attention and live it well, it can become deformed into grotesque results. Needs, as I have previously stated, are relational and have to be presented as invitations to relationship in order to be tended to well.

The more we offer our selves, the more often we have to be refilled.

The more we pour out of our selves in meeting the needs of others in our personal and professional lives, the more we must recognize our own needs to be replenished. In our passion to offer our love and gifts, we can spread our selves over great distances or into great depths, so to speak. This offering, whether from a mother or father, mayor or machinist, leaves the person tired, worn, and even empty. This person needs attention—more than the child, because the child is depending on the parent to have something to give. Any person who pours out is going to wind up needing to be refilled. The more we offer our selves, the more often we have to be refilled. So, acknowledging our need to be tended to means that we are being responsible grown-ups. Needing attention means that we value ourselves and value what we do. It is not shameful.

Attention comes from our selves, others, and in quiet moments of meditation and prayer with God. I believe that a person who expends a lot of his or her energy in life as a servant needs about two hours a day of attention. After hearing me offer this statement people often exclaim: "What are you talking about? That's more work!" While on the surface it literally is more time spent, I believe that when our need for attention is sufficiently met, our ability to be present creates more time. When we are well tended to, we are more capable of participating fully in the time we have, rather than wishing we could escape into distractions from our lives. Our part of being tended to involves: getting up earlier, spending time journaling, praying, taking care of our bodies, asking for our needs to be met, asking for help, recognizing encouragement, and listening to the beat of our emotional hearts and the images of our dreams.

Perhaps most importantly, we need to know who the people are that we can call. We need to know those people who will care about us, because they accept us as a burden in their lives. That is correct. Love is a burden, and we are made to burden people with it. If we hate being burdens, then we are not going to be good at getting attention. If we hate being burdens, we are not going to be good at accepting that we have needs. If we are not willing to be a burden of love or bear the burden of love, then, ironically, we are actually going to become a weight that will crush the people we say we care about. People who deny their needs can be very destructive to relationships and love.

CHAPTER 8

SEXUALITY

℃℞

The need for sexuality has nothing to do with the action of sex. The need of sexuality is our need to feel and experience comfort and confidence in our own skin. Sexuality fulfillment is the feeling of being glad to be in our skin. Sexuality is the experience of gladness, confidence, and comfort in our male or female skin. When the need for sexuality is met, it travels from our hearts all the way out to our faces. We can be ourselves. We are not hiding our hearts out of the fear of rejection by our own kind. Being comfortable and confident in our own skin allows us to continue to be good at asking for what we need from others like us. If you are a man, you know that you need encouragement and care, tenderness and teaching from other men, because men know what it is like to be one. If you are a woman, you know that you need encouragement and care, tenderness and teaching from other women, because women know what it is like to be one. Basically, you and I have permission, without regard for graded performance, to be fully present with our own kind, who can influence our hearts to continue growing into who we are made to be.

If we are not comfortable being in need, having the confidence in being our selves, then we have to hide who we are. In my 30 years of working predominately with men and married couples, I have seen over and over again how we (men and women) tend to hide our vulnerabilities behind some form of performance power—when men are with men, and women are with women—which blocks the fulfillment of sexuality need. Performance power sends a double-message: (1) It communicates denial of your neediness through a self-sufficiency cure that is marked by invulnerability, i.e., you are superior. (2) While also stating that you are on equal footing with all others, i.e., you are humble. This control/false humility dynamic of distrust within a woman's or man's interactions causes relational difficulty and confusion.

Sexuality is the experience of gladness, confidence, and comfort in our own skin.

It presents a mask of superiority to others by being the one who does not need and, usually, communicates an unspoken recognition that vulnerability is not tolerated, unless the one in need is accepting the, usually unspoken, rules or "fixes" of the superior person. This same man, who cannot allow other men to meet him in his neediness, will often attempt to get a woman (especially spouse) to meet their masculine needs, and a woman cannot do it. This same woman, who cannot allow other women to meet her in her neediness, will do the same.

Tragedy lies within this dynamic. Men will demand that their wives become praising-pampering-pitying mothers and/or nameless mistresses instead of women in their own greatness. Women will demand that their husbands become adoring-permissive-fixing daddies and/or unattached philandering, irresponsible boys instead of men in their own greatness. The greatness is the capacity for passion, the ability for intimacy, and the dependability of integrity. Without this greatness, men and women who will not admit their neediness, raise children to be unaccepting of their own neediness, so they end up covering over their needs, too.

If we are comfortable and confident being male or female, then we will be able to extend and stretch ourselves into other territories because we are not afraid of losing ourselves. In other words, men can bring out what is traditionally thought of as femininity without fear (because of confidence). Obviously, the opposite can be said for women. For example, what is traditionally thought of as feminine is a man's tenderness, touch, nurture, care, thoughtfulness, and kindness to other people. What is traditionally thought of as masculine is a woman's toughness, reserve, willingness to risk, sacrifice of life, and ability to be separate. If men are unable to display both feminine and masculine traits with each other, true friendship and love will never be able to flourish. Performance power will fester and destroy the possibility for relationship, not only with each other, but also between men and women.

Sexuality need is grown through the affirmation and confirmation of important caregivers who say we belong and matter, as we bring our feelings, needs, desire, longings and hope to the heart of our lived experience. For those of us whose sexuality need was harmed, it can be rebuilt by today's caregivers who are in healing and now walk in their greatness.

Of course, each need discussed in these descriptions leaves much unstated. In spite of this reality, let me end this sexuality need section with a large hope for each of us. Every person needs six pallbearers; that is, every person needs friends to walk through the journey of the heart with. These people will miss us terribly when we depart, because they knew us and they carry our story with them from the inside-out. Anybody can carry a casket, but it takes a friend to honor the life we had. One of the ways we meet our "pallbearers" is to have our need for sexuality met, which leads us to be all of who we are, and to walk confidently in being fully known.

CHAPTER 9

GUIDANCE

CR

We also have a need for guidance, from birth to death, which helps us become guides to others as they travel the same journey each of us inevitably takes. The question is not whether each of us survives the journey, but the quality with which we live our time on Earth. In order to live the experience of life well, we have to have others show us how to do it. Guidance shows us how to go where we have never been in life: How do we be fathers/mothers? How do we move into a career? How do we stay connected to God when life turns away from dreams? How do we pay for school or go on vacation? How do we talk to children? How do we heal from trauma? How do we die? How do we live?

The number of times we have been through life is how many times? Everything I know about my life says once. So, this is our first time through life. Being able to receive guidance begins with neediness. Of course we are in need of being guided! This is the first time we have lived. We have to learn how to live where we are. How do we grow? We only grow through asking the questions that neediness arouses. We must take a stance of dependence toward another person who has something we don't have: life experience, wisdom, kindness, etc.

The need for guidance begins with being able to be dependent on others to meet our needs. Being guided towards wherever we need to go by trusted others and God begins with wondering out loud, so we can find out that which we don't know and can't know without asking. Asking questions, experimenting with trial and error, seeking information from other people, and learning through experience are all ways we learn how to explore the world in order to become competent in living. Trusted others have to guide us, because it's our first time being alive. We need somebody who is 30 to tell us how to be 30. And as we're going towards 50, 60, 70, 80, we need to be able to ask others: What's it like to be 80? What's it like to be 70? What's it like to be 40? I use ages to represent times of future needs.

Unfortunately, we're often ashamed of needing guidance. An acronym for God that is relevant to the need for guidance is: Good Orderly Direction (G. O. D.). Do you realize that we have to be bigger than G. O. D. if we are unable or unwilling to ask questions? We become haters of good orderly direction through being shamed and harmed for asking and needing help. Those of us who reject guidance, literally and narcissistically expect our selves, armed with our grandiose beliefs, to be able to know everything without ever having asked questions and learned from others and God. When we start digging into needs, we find that the logic we have used to deny neediness is insane. However, if we apply honesty, openness, and willingness (H.O.W.) to good orderly direction (G.O.D.), we diminish our egos (Easing God Out) and find ourselves in a full life.

Initially, asking for help remains difficult when we re-awaken to our needs and engage them in Circles of Security. It is going to be embarrassing; being human will always remain an embarrassing experience because we have a picture of perfection. Laughter with others who get that reality is very helpful.

We must continue to rediscover and surrender to the reality that we are emotional and spiritual creatures—not slugs, raccoons, rats, birds, or scorpions. Do you get it? Those things get by on essential provisional existence. We're made for more than provisional existence. We're made to live fully. We're made for more than survival and instinct. We are created to be guided and to guide. We cannot give what we do not have; therefore, we must be guided well. In that way a parent's words of wisdom can answer to a child who needs to know how to live the journey of life, which will always call us to neediness. We need to become good at asking questions and being guided by others who have gone before us.

CHAPTER 10

ACCOMPLISHMENT

☙

The need for accomplishment sounds like we finally get to bring our products to the group and get praised for them, doesn't it? True accomplishment is not what popular culture tells us it is. The need for accomplishment is not about experiencing fullness through achievements. Accomplishment, contrary to popular thought, starts with the recognition of our limitations. We have a desire to do well, create, and achieve. The need of accomplishment being attended to allows "doing well" to occur. True accomplishment is fulfilled through a three-step process: (1) knowing when you have reached marginal diminishing returns and stopping; (2) celebrating the result of having given yourself to something that matters to you; (3) and resting well to allow you to begin anew as you move towards the "completion" of that which moves us. When we know our need of accomplishment, we know when we need to stop, we can be grateful for what has happened so far, and we can rest well in anticipation instead of dread.

Marginal diminishing returns mean that if we go any farther, we are continuing to work out of sheer determination, rather than out of creative passion. The energy applied to the work actually reduces productivity and, even more so, quality. The person who taught me a great deal about the need for accomplishment was a guy who built a stone wall in our house as part of its construction years ago. He cut and carved every stone with extreme care. This man was an artist. One day I saw him sitting and staring at the unfinished rock wall. As I approached, he said to me, "The rocks aren't talking to me today." He then added, "The man upstairs picks 'em, not me." At this point, I'm thinking, "Just do the wall!" The mason then said, "I gotta go." He had only placed four rocks that day. This man knew the need of accomplishment, and I did not. I wanted him to push through and finish the wall out of sheer willpower. Thankfully, he knew what it meant to accomplish. Accomplishment means that he looked at those rocks and said, "I'm not in it today. I can't do it." Instead of betraying himself, he left and came back the next day ready to begin anew.

Accomplishment starts with the recognition of our limitations.

When he finished the wall—and he did finish the wall—he took me on a tour of what he had created. He literally talked about different stones and their part in the wall. He even said, pointing to one stone, "a child will someday run their fingers along these rivers of markings that lead to the next stone." Because he knew his limitations, he knew when to stop and rest, which returned him to creativity. This awareness and response allowed him to have a larger celebration with me when he finished. Part of his celebration was taking me on a tour of the wall. The wall, this person's creation, was alive for him in ways I wouldn't have understood if he had not celebrated his accomplishment with me. He was an artist who knew his art well, and he knew his need for accomplishment, which led him to the completion of his creative tasks. He did the process of accomplishment naturally, probably without needing the description I am offering here; however, I do believe that he would nod in approval about the description stated above.

So, the best way for us to engage creatively with our lives is to recognize our limitations, celebrate how much we have invested/participated/grown, and rest well in order to begin again. The need of accomplishment allows us to live the daily circle of life, and attend also to the greater, larger circle of life that we are all created to participate in.

CHAPTER 11

SUPPORT

CR

The need for support is a thread that runs throughout all the other needs. However, until we move into awareness of the above-mentioned needs, support does not stand out as a vibrant need. As a way to distinguish it from the other needs, I define support as the need for continual responding to and replenishment of my ongoing needs. Basically, the need of support is met by my ability to call upon others and God to meet me in my present condition—celebration/grief or offering/receiving—knowing that I can have confidence in their response. I live knowing that I am not self-sufficient; I am not going to find a self-cure for neediness; and addiction robs me of the life of sensitivity and creativity I was created to live. I will always have the need of others in my ongoing daily life. The struggle of living is a daily experience. Support gives us confidence for daily life.

Meeting the need of support begins with the daily acknowledgment that we are unable to live fully by ourselves. We must be responsible for our lives, but we cannot do life alone. Questions related to the need for support are: Are you with me? Are you in my corner? Do you care about me? Are you praying for me? We need to know there is somebody out there that cares about what happens to us. And we need to become people who can offer as much as we have received.

Support gives us confidence for daily life.

A very painful awakening occurred in me years ago when I was sitting in my car at an intersection in Texas during a boom time, when the sprawl of the city had stretched out to take in sold-out farmland. There was a herd of cattle on one corner and a two-thousand unit luxury apartment complex on the other corner. I remember being struck by how absolutely alone I felt. There was no one I could call to talk to about my internal world, and I needed to desperately. If all of a sudden I got T-boned at that intersection, I feared that no one in my life would have ever known me and that no one around me would care what happened to me. I was not known from within at the time by really anyone. My addiction to self-sufficiency anesthetized the need in me to have someone to know me and care right then. However, it could not fully silence, ultimately, my neediness. I had no support in my life, no one to contact to say how scared or alone I felt. Through this experience I began to awaken. I began to work towards a neediness that has brought me and others many, many good things in this life. We are not made to live alone.

CHAPTER 12

LISTENING & TRUST

☙

The need for listening involves needing others to give their hearts to us while we speak about the parts of our lives that matter most to us, whether they are daily life occurrences or deep mysteries of days past. The need for trust fulfills the anticipated dependability of the person who is listening. If we don't ever take the risk of talking, of sharing what is going on in our hearts with others we hope will be present and truthful, then we will never feel listened to and fully cared about. In turn, we lose strength, become distant or defensive, judgmental or isolated, and then the world ultimately loses a listening ear and a dependable heart. The world loses you or me.

Being listened to involves having a need for someone to see us while we talk; their faces register our own internal experiences, as much as our faces move when we see boxing or experience a funny scene. This "facing" and "showing," lets the person talking know that we are in the story that they are telling. When the need of listening is met, the speaker becomes open to hearing the listener share their experience of what was heard. The one who has been heard is likely to trust the person who listened. In other words, the one who experiences being listened to will be more likely to trust feedback, even when it does not agree with the speaker. When someone is with us in their heart, their faces match what is going on in their hearts, and the words spoken are directly connected with what was heard.

To have someone meet the need of listening allows us to have the need of trust fulfilled at the same time. Trust allows us to risk our hearts, because we believe the other is dependable in heart to be truthful.

Trust allows us to risk our hearts.

At a point in my father's medical career, he decided to start "telling the truth" to patients after listening very closely to all of their words and symptoms. There was an 80-something year old female patient of his who was dying of cancer. After multiple treatment attempts, he knew that the woman would die. He asked the husband to be present in the room, and he told the couple of 56 years that death was inevitable and would be soon. He said their names and then continued with, "There's nothing we can do. We've done everything that can be done. I don't know when she will die, but your wife's going to die. And it's probably going to be soon. Whatever peace you need to make with each other, you need to do so, starting now." He then told them that he was so sorry, as he left the room and them to their endings.

He told me that he was just about 20 feet down the hallway and heard, "Doc, Doc, hold on, Doc." The husband approached my father, reached out to hold his arm and said, "Doc, Doc, listen to me now. Thank you. You are just like a Daddy to me. Thank you for being someone I can trust." He was 80-something years old, 25 years older than my own father. "You're just like a Daddy to me. Thank you," the old man said. He then turned around and pattered back into the room to be with his spouse. That couple was in great need of someone competent and caring to listen deeply to their needs, so they could trust someone to be deeply interested in their welfare. My father met them in it, and he himself was rewarded by being heard and told that he was trustworthy. The guidance the couple was able to receive from him occurred through the power of listening and trust.

You, the reader, will clearly see, if you have not already, that the needs work in a concert of connection. By one need being met, many others are also touched at the same time.

CHAPTER 13

FREEDOM

☙

We are born to be free. Freedom means being liberated from the tyranny that stops us from living fully, loving deeply, and leading well lives that others can be thankful for. This liberation offers the freedom to create and give to a world in need—or not. Freedom can also be used tragically to attempt to run away from our selves. Freedom actually is the opportunity of being liberated from having to run away from who we are created to be and what we are created to do. We don't need to go to Europe, buy a Harley, start a band, or be famous to be our selves. We may need to take action in these ways, however, to express the creativity of who we are and in order to offer to others what we are made to do. Nevertheless, there is no such place as away, if we think that "away" will free us from the "bondage" of self, or free us from the gift and responsibility of living who we are.

The need for freedom is our need to be liberated from anything that would stop us from becoming who we were born to be. The self we are made to be is waiting within us at all times, ready to be expressed. "Away" becomes how far we run from this reality. We were born to remain emotional and spiritual creatures. Hence, when we have the recognition of our needs, we are also committing ourselves to a revolution against the powers that tell us otherwise about our needs and our selves.

A revolution of liberty (not a rebellion of discontent) must be waged for us to become our true selves, instead of what the powers that would reduce us to *things* would have us become. Sometimes the powers are the parents. Sometimes the powers are the teachers. Sometimes the power is what we do to our selves. For example, we threaten our selves, call our selves names, and "should" on our selves for being human and in need. The recovery of our need for freedom ultimately lets us live the liberation from the bondage of our own egos. Ego, which can stand for easing God out (E.G.O.), involves fancying ourselves as self-sufficient gods, so we will not have needs, be vulnerable, and never be fooled or have to hurt again. Ego is the face we put on to hide the vulnerability and greatness of the human heart. Ego enslaves; selfhood sets us free. We become free to be responsible, take risks, and face our choices. We are not under someone else's control when we are free.

We are going to hurt in our freedom, for sure. Remember that we are made to feel hurt so we can heal and renew courage to live. Nobody climbs a mountain unless they know there is a possibility that they will fall. No one uses their freedom to live fully without knowing that pain is part of the living. Being liberated involves being free to express our selves related either to finishing the climb or not being able to finish. We are created to seek whatever is true, noble, right, pure, lovely, admirable, excellent, or praiseworthy. Likewise, we are created to see and feel how far we are from these genuine desires and longings; and we are free to grieve the pains of loss.

CHAPTER 14

FUN

☙

The need for fun doesn't involve being entertained in order to distract our selves. Fun gives us rest and re-creation. In fun, we rest from toil and experience the re-creation that creativity brings to us. And we do not even know we are doing it when we are doing it! True fun involves being fully human and not being conscious about it. In fun, we are not forgetting our selves; we are being our selves completely. Afterwards, we may look back upon the experience and see/recall what we received.

A child flying a kite is a small and wonderful picture of what fun is and what it does. A child runs so that the kite may fly, watches it lift into the air, lets it dive and twirl, and finally stares into the wonder of the sky and earth. That child is not thinking: "I wonder how my hair looks when I run; I wonder if people are watching me run with it; I wonder if I look good running; I bet they think I'm stupid." The child is not, in a sense, thinking, or at the least, not actively registering their thoughts. They are capable of participating in the simple beauty of flying a kite, rather than thinking about anything else. They are completely not conscious of their consciousness. They are "gone" into life and living, fully participating in the work of life —giving hands, head, and heart over to living and doing it with courage, which means the heart is fully engaged and participating. They are replenishing themselves and bonding with life by disappearing into the midst of it. And, again, they do not know it. The rest and continuing re-creation of living has occurred.

We have to have these moments of un-self-consciousness; otherwise, life is not full of its worth. It is all labor, as opposed to work. Labor is when we must block our existence to survive, versus work, which is fully participating in our existence because hope is alive and vibrant, even in difficult circumstances. We have to be able to stop. We have to be able to release our selves to hope and all of its imaginative possibilities. If we do not do so, we eventually become dry husks of survival.

True fun involves being fully human and not being conscious about it.

If we do not continue to become skilled at being needy, then I think we lose our true selves. Because we are created to live, we are going to live; whether through survival or thriving, we live. Fun allows a person to forget consciousness of self, by giving over to something greater than the self. We give our selves to wonder. If we do not release our selves to wonder, we survive through anxiety and its hyper-vigilant demands, which continually block any expression that reveals the true vulnerability of needing.

While the needs to belong and matter are the foundational needs upon which we build our vulnerable lives, I believe that the need of fun is the capstone. I think, perhaps, that all the other needs lie between the foundation we build upon—belonging and mattering—while we live the lives, full of pain and tragedy, of course, that we are created to have—fun.

CONCLUSION

ᴄᴙ

In closing this writing on needs, I recognize that the list is not exhaustive. I am aware that life contains so much more that we both know and do not know. However, we do know that humans are created to need, whether we like it or not. We are dependent upon how we are made, dependent on each other, and dependent on God, whether we like it or not. We have feelings, which lead us to needs—no matter what we do to ward them off or minimize there impact, whether we like it or not (and I often do not!). We also know that when human beings face neediness, dependence, and feelings, we have a tendency to find the life we had forgotten we could have.

About the Author
CHIP DODD

☙

Chip Dodd, PhD, is a teacher, trainer, author, and counselor, who has been working in the field of recovery and redemption for over 30 years. It is the territory in which people can return to living the way we are created to live—where we can move from mere survival to living fully, from isolation to loving deeply, and from controlling to leading others well.

In 1996 after receiving his PhD in counseling from the University of North Texas, Chip founded a treatment center in Nashville, TN, where he continues the work of helping patients recover full living.

With his clinical experience, love of storytelling, and passion for living fully, Chip developed a way of seeing and expressing one's internal experience called the Spiritual Root System™. It expresses the essential heart of human beings and gives practical tools to live fully, love deeply, and lead well.

ALSO BY CHIP DODD:
The Voice of the Heart
Anthem to the Invisible
The Perfect Loss: A Different Kind of Happiness
Live Fully: Meditations on Passion
Love Deeply: Meditations on Intimacy
Lead Well: Meditations on Integrity
Available online at www.sagehillresources.com

About

SAGE HILL

☙

Sage Hill is a social impact organization founded by Chip Dodd, committed to helping others see who they are made to be so they can do what they are made to do.

Wherever life has you, we're here to help you keep heart. We offer recovery and addiction treatment programs, therapeutic counseling, leadership development intensives, corporate consulting, staff retreats, teaching resources, and more. Visit us online for more information.

SAGE HILL RECOVERY.COM

The Center for Professional Excellence (CPE), is a multidisciplinary treatment center for professional men who want to recover their lives, their passions, and their integrity from the effects of addiction, depression, anxiety, and other behavioral problems.

SAGE HILL INSTITUTE.ORG

Sage Hill Institute exists to provide encouragement, education, support, and accountability for leaders using the Spiritual Root System™. We provide leadership development, team building, spiritual and emotional healing, and other services to support the viability of a leader's calling.

SAGE HILL COUNSELING.COM

When life doesn't work, Sage Hill Counseling is here to help. We offer counseling for individuals, couples, families, children/adolescents, and group therapies to help you heal, grow, and mature. Sage Hill Counseling centers are currently located in Nashville, TN and Memphis, TN.

SAGE HILL RESOURCES.COM

Sage Hill Resources is dedicated to producing materials that help you keep heart. All of our resources use the wisdom of the Spiritual Root System™ to help you gain a deeper understanding of your heart, which can lead to more authentic relationship with yourself, others, and God.

SAGE HILL
A SOCIAL IMPACT ORGANIZATION

Wake up and go home to who you are made to be.

The
VOICE OF THE HEART

THE VOICE OF THE HEART
Second Edition

SECOND EDITION
with Companion Bible Study

In 2001, *The Voice of the Heart* began a steady journey into the lives of those looking for more. Since its initial release, *The Voice of the Heart* has been handed one friend to another and has helped thousands of people begin to speak the truth of their story and to live more fully from the heart.

Available online at www.sagehillresources.com

The
PERFECT LOSS

A Different Kind of Happiness

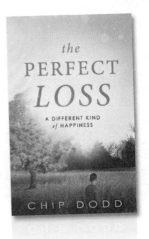

Through the use of story, experience, knowledge, and Scripture, we follow Chip Dodd as he shows us how to walk the path toward a life of passion, intimacy and integrity—leaving a legacy that passes life forward to those we love and beyond.

Though the fig tree does not bud and there are no grapes on the vines, though the olive crop fails and the fields produce no food, though there are no sheep in the pen and no cattle in the stalls, yet I will rejoice in the LORD.

—Habakkuk 3:17-18

Using the Beatitudes, the author shows us the eight movements we all must make if we are to live fully.

Available online at www.sagehillresources.com

ANTHEM TO THE INVISIBLE

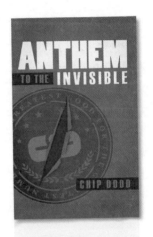

Anthem to the Invisible tells the story of a man who has lost his way, trying to change a world he cannot change. His intellect convinces no one and his ego has imprisoned him. He then does what he thought he would never do: walks away from the Collective.

While he thought he had lost everything he had given his life to, he instead discovers that he has awakened to his true self. His journey takes him places he had hoped he would never see in this dystopian society, a world where savagery is emerging and cold-blooded decisions are taking over. The spiritual and material worlds have collided, leaving him in a war of love. He fights for the heart and finds himself, his people, and love.

Available online at www.sagehillresources.com

STAY INSPIRED,
KEEP HEART

Connect with Sage Hill

sagehillinstitute.com/keepingheart

Facebook.com/chipdoddphd & Facebook.com/sagehillinstitute

@chipdodd & @sage_hill

sagehillinstitute.com/podcast

vimeo.com/chipdodd

Find daily inspiration, stay current on Sage Hill events, gain
access to free videos, podcasts and more.

Subscribe online at www.chipdodd.com

NOTES

NOTES

NOTES

NOTES

NOTES

NOTES